THE AFTERMATH OF BETRAYAL

MICHELLE D. MAYS LPC, CSAT-S

RELATIONAL RECOVERY PRESS

~

To the women of the PartnerHope focus group. For your courageous hope in the face of daunting circumstances and your desire to light a pathway for those who come behind you.

INTRODUCTION

Betrayal shatters your world. In a moment, everything you thought you knew and could count on changes. The person closest to you switches in an instant from your deepest source of safety and connection to a source of pain, fear and emotional danger.

This is the experience of betrayal trauma. For betrayed partners in the middle of this chaotic, fragmenting, and devastating experience, the whole world is turned upside down and everything feels uncertain.

One of the first ways to help yourself with betrayal trauma is to recognize and put into words the felt experience you are going through. This helps you begin the process of understanding and integrating what has happened into the narrative of your life.

The goal of this book is to help you identify and articulate the experience you are having—to give you words, language, and concepts to describe this storm of betrayal. My hope is that you will then be able to share about your experience with your support system in ways they can understand and feel.

This is incredibly important, because sharing your experience with empathetic others will help you to feel less alone on your journey. Other people have been where you are and understand the frightening experience of betrayal trauma. When you share your story with them, you are in wise and caring company.

Years ago, I went through my own story of betrayal trauma. I was married to a man who was sexually addicted and journeyed through all the feelings, behaviors, and experiences that I talk about in this book. I went from the initial discovery of betrayal through the winding road of recovery and eventually to a place of great healing and restoration. This book is not theory. It is lived experience and is written from my heart to yours wherever you are on your journey.

So, let's get started. This book is divided into six chapters of varying lengths that each look at a certain aspect of betrayal trauma's impact. These different elements are not linear. You will find yourself experiencing many at once, and bouncing from one to another again and again.

At the end of each chapter there is a FOR YOUR CONSIDERATION section that offers Journal Prompts and Exercises that can help you process the experience of betrayal trauma. Feel free to do them or not do them. Pick out the ones that appeal to you and do them first. Follow your sense of which ones will help you the most and focus on those. This is your journey, so listen closely to and trust your inner wisdom about what you need.

Please be aware that as you put words to the experience of betrayal trauma you may feel great relief; finally, someone is helping you name what is happening. You may also have strong and overwhelming feelings of anger, fear, shame, etc. The process of articulating the impact of betrayal trauma brings these feelings into sharper focus. This is not always pleasant, but it's necessary if you want to heal. In time, you will process your feelings in ways that allow them to move through you. When this occurs, you heal.

The information provided in this book is intended to help educate and offer support to individuals dealing with the trauma of betrayal. Every person's story of betrayal is different and unique. This book does not address all the many specific and varied details that can be present in the aftermath of betrayal. In addition, this book is not intended as a substitute for treatment by a trained and licensed mental health professional. Please seek professional advice, help and support if you are dealing with betrayal.

Given all that may come up as you read, you will want to go slow and take your time. Breathe, take breaks, take naps, walk your dog, be kind to yourself, and breathe some more. You are at the beginning of the healing process, and kindness and care for yourself are essential right now.

REALITY FRAGMENTATION

*D*iscovering your partner's secret sexual behavior is one of the most shocking experiences of betrayal you can have. Whether it is an affair or a long-term pattern of sexual acting out, the sheer devastation of finding out your partner is not who you thought he or she was, and your relationship is not what you thought it was, can suck the emotional wind out of you. When you combine the discovery of your partner's sexual behaviors with the experience of being lied to and manipulated, the trauma compounds and becomes even more severe.

Initially, many partners can't believe that what they are seeing or hearing is real. They think: How can this be happening? Has the person I loved, lived with, and built a life alongside really been lying to me this way? Has my partner truly betrayed me in such a heartrending and shocking manner?

The first experience most betrayed partners have is disbelief. They struggle to wrap their mind around the betrayal and to comprehend what has happened. They experience a profound sense of disorientation as they are forced to integrate information that completely alters their understanding of reality. A client recently said to me, "I kept trying to accept in my head that what I was seeing was real. But I couldn't get it to stay there. My mind wanted to reject it."

The Fragmenting of Reality

This experience of struggling to comprehend what has happened is called Reality Fragmentation. Reality Fragmentation is when you discover that the reality you thought you were living is a fiction. Instead, you have been living in an entirely separate reality, but you didn't know it.

One of my clients who is in this early stage of Reality Fragmentation keeps saying to me, "My husband and I had a great marriage. We were emotionally connected, we were intimate, we had hot sex, and we were madly in love with each other. How could he have been disconnected and distracted without me knowing it? It doesn't make sense."

Meanwhile, she has learned that when she met her husband he was actively engaged in compulsive sexual behaviors outside of the relationship. He was looking at porn obsessively, seeing prostitutes, sexting with random people online, and visiting massage parlors.

For this client, the emotional connection with her husband felt real and better than any previous relationship she had experienced. She thought they were deeply bonded, faithful to one another, and safe and secure in their relational and romantic connection. When she discovered his secret sexual life, it threw everything she thought she knew into chaos. Now she is in the process of revisiting her relationship and trying to understand what has happened. She asks: "How could I have felt so safely connected while my husband was spending hours each day acting out? How could I have thought he was present with me, attentive, and on the same relational page, when all along he had a secret sexual life?"

Hall of Mirrors

For betrayed partners, Reality Fragmentation is like living in a hall of mirrors. Each mirror holds a fragment, but the fragments don't seem to relate to each other or make sense. One mirror holds an image of your spouse with a prostitute. Another mirror holds a picture of the two of you making love and feeling deeply intimate. A third mirror holds an image of conversations you had about your goals and dreams. A fourth mirror holds an image of compulsive porn use and masturbation. A fifth mirror holds an image of your partner as a good parent. Etc. After discovery, you can find yourself trapped in this hall of mirrors with no way to make sense of the fragmented lies and betrayals.

Complicating matters is the fact that you might not get the truth all at once. Instead, it may trickle out over time. For instance, your partner might tell you the affair was just an emotional relationship. Then he might confess that yes, there was sex, but just one time. Later, he may disclose that the affair was sexual for over six months, with daily contact. This trickle of information increases your disorientation. As soon as sense is made of the current information, another round of data floods in, washing away the previous version of the truth and sweeping you back into fragmented chaos.

One of the most emotionally damaging things one person can do to another is to make that person doubt his or her ability to perceive reality accurately. Reality Fragmentation and the resulting disorientation causes betrayed partners to feel as if they are losing their minds. A betrayed partner reflecting back on this early stage told me, "I thought I was going crazy. I thought that I was truly going insane."

When you are in a situation that is destabilizing to your emotional, physical, and mental functioning, trusting anyone becomes very challenging. While desperately looking for some solid ground to stand on in the middle of the quicksand your life has become, it is difficult to know who to turn to for advice and emotional support. After all, you thought you were on solid ground before, and that turned out to be a sinkhole. So now it feels almost impossible to trust your partner, others, or even yourself.

Help and Support

However, getting help during this time is critical. You need support, wisdom, care and kindness from sources outside of yourself. The following are some suggested ways to care for yourself in the midst of Reality Fragmentation.

- Finding a trained therapist with expertise in the typical stages individuals and couples go through in the aftermath of betrayal is important. I recommend that you look for a therapist who understands the ways in which your capacity to trust has been damaged and can help you manage your Reality Fragmentation. Be cautious of therapists who want to rush to repair the relationship before the whole story of betrayal has been disclosed. This can result in further wounding and increased distrust, not only with your partner but with the therapist who pushed for vulnerability before it was safe to do so.

- Finding a therapist trained in treating sexual addiction can be helpful. Certified Sex Addiction Therapists (CSATs) have extensive training in how to handle the first stages after discovery. They are also trained to help couples give and receive a full disclosure of the secret behaviors in a way that minimizes harm. Moreover, they can screen for the presence of sexually compulsive behavior, helping to determine whether you are dealing with infidelity, sexual addiction, love addiction, or some other issue.

- In addition to finding trained and experienced help, it is important to find safe friends to talk to. One of the ways to leave the hall of mirrors is by sorting out truth from lies. Talking through what has happened, what you know, and what you are finding out with friends who will listen and offer nonjudgmental support is incredibly important during this time.

- Another way to sort through what has happened is to journal. During this emotionally painful time, it is easy to become confused and not remember pieces of information. Writing things down provides a record to refer back to. The process of writing also slows your mind in ways that help you remember the truth. Plus, journaling gives you a place to pour out all the emotions streaming through you, and to put into words your answers to the big questions that inevitably arise during this stage.

My last suggestion for helping with Reality Fragmentation is that you open yourself up to learning new information and thinking about things in new ways. To illustrate, let's return for a moment to the client I mentioned above, the woman who just learned her relationship is not what she thought it was.

This individual has a narrative that she has been telling herself about her, her spouse, and their love story for a very long time. Now this narrative no longer makes sense. It doesn't add up when she considers the other part of the story—the secret part that she didn't know about before. Now she is faced with having to let go of her narrative, which means letting go of something that felt certain and predictable. She has to figure out what the real story is. She needs to know and accept what has truly been occurring between her and her spouse.

If she clings to her old narrative and does not find a way to open up and ask difficult questions, she will never learn what has really been happening in the relationship. She will miss out on discovering that there is a level of connection and secure bonding available in relationships that she has not experienced before, and that she and her spouse can experience if they heal. Most importantly, she will miss out on learning about herself and growing in ways that bring new freedoms and joy into her life.

While it is always scary to leave behind something that felt certain or at least familiar, it is the letting go that opens space for something new to come in. Often, that new thing can change the course of life in good and surprising ways.

~

FOR YOUR CONSIDERATION

Journal Prompt
Describe how it felt to be in your relationship before you experienced betrayal trauma.

Describe how it feels to be in your relationship after experiencing betrayal trauma. What is different for you today?

Reality Fragmentation Mosaic Exercise
Because betrayed partners experience Reality Fragmentation along with shock and states of bodily overwhelm, it can be challenging to hold on to information that has surfaced or to remember the things that have occurred. The mind can skip and jump, making it difficult to piece together a coherent narrative that you can absorb and integrate into your experience. This exercise is designed to help you capture the scraps of information flying through your mind, and to form them into a whole picture and story that you can start to process. If you find yourself getting overwhelmed, consider doing this exercise in your therapist's office with his or her support.

- Take a large piece of blank paper and tear it into a bunch of smaller pieces. On each piece of paper write down one of the fragments of new information that you have learned. Just write down the facts you know, not things you suspect or fear. Once you have written each fact on a piece of the paper, spread them out on the floor and take some time to look at them. What do you notice? What information are these different fragments telling you? Are you learning anything new? What is getting clearer for you? Are there pieces that belong together in a group?

- Now take more blank scraps of paper, and on each scrap write an emotion that you are feeling about the information in front of you (sad, angry, confused, betrayed, horrified, scared, etc.) Place these scraps in a circle around the pieces with information on them. When you are finished, sit back and look at the picture you have created and visually absorb it. What are you learning? What feelings are coming up?

- Some betrayed partners, when they see this picture take shape, feel relieved because the betrayal starts to feel contained. The picture has edges and is knowable and nameable. The pieces of the story begin to feel pinned down instead of floating free in a racing, tumbling mess. What is your reaction to seeing the story contained on the paper in front of you?

- For other betrayed partners, this picture helps them see the gaps between what they know and what they don't know. It helps them identify the places that don't make sense. While that can feel scary, it also helps them to know that there is more information they need from their significant other. Are there any gaps that you are identifying as you look at the picture in front of you?

- Once you have completed this exercise, either get a large piece of paper that you can glue the mosaic to, or take a picture of it. You will want to be able to refer back to it when you feel disconnected or are spinning with Reality Fragmentation. You may also want to add to it if new information is revealed as you go forward.

2

THE PROTECTIVE FOG OF SHOCK

*A*my and Jacob have been married for 15 years. Amy found out about Jacob's sexual behaviors when he was arrested for having sex in a public restroom at an amusement park. They entered therapy and began to learn about sexual addiction and recovery. Early in the therapy process, we had a couple's session and Jacob told Amy about more of his secret sexual behaviors. In addition to the incident in the amusement park, he revealed several more affairs and one-time sexual encounters over a span of years.

As Amy listened, I could see her shut down and enter the protective fog of shock. The information was too painful to absorb. As she became overwhelmed, her body came to the rescue and put a buffer between her and what she was hearing. She asked some questions, but mostly sat in silence with tears streaming down her face.

Shock is the brain's way of protecting us from information and events that are too overwhelming to deal with in the moment. For instance, a person who suddenly loses a loved one will often go into shock. A protective cloud will envelop that person, numbing their feelings and holding the implications of their loved one's death at bay until they can absorb what has happened. This type of protective fog lets them get out of bed, shower and get dressed, answer questions about funeral arrangements, attend the funeral, and interact with family and friends. It helps them function when otherwise they might collapse.

This same type of protective shock often envelops betrayed partners after discovering infidelity.

During therapy over the next few weeks, Amy asked questions about Jacob's sexual behaviors. I gently reminded her that he had already given her the answers. She looked at me with startled disbelief. As I reminded her of what she had heard, she slumped into herself saying, "Oh yeah," as she recognized and remembered the information. This happened repeatedly over many sessions because she truly couldn't remember. Her brain had blocked out the information because it was too painful. Slowly, over time, she was able to let the blocked information come in and begin to process it.

Shock can also create a sense of being gone from your body. One of my clients talked about not knowing how she got her daughter to the bus stop or how she got to the grocery store. She was going through the motions of life but was not present or aware.

In whatever way it manifests, shock can last from a couple of weeks to a few months depending on the person and the circumstances. The feeling of being lost in a fog can come and go at the beginning, with some days feeling emotionally cloudier and other days feeling clearer.

When Shock Begins to Lift

When shock begins to wear off, there is a thawing of emotions and feelings start to be felt and processed. You may notice that instead of your grief, anger, and pain feeling slightly separate from you or a bit fuzzy, they are suddenly engulfing you and being felt in vivid color. Tears that felt stuck or unable to fully flow may now arrive in unpredictable torrents. The feeling of walking around half asleep or on autopilot may be replaced by feeling highly charged, disorganized, and hyper-vigilant. These are all signs that the protective fog of shock is receding.

You may recognize your version of shock and wonder: *What do I do about this?* The answer is nothing. Shock is your body's way of protecting you, and this protective fog will eventually diminish, allowing you to more fully connect to and process your new reality. This will happen naturally, over time, as your system adjusts.

If, after several weeks or months, you continue to feel like you are stuck in shock, talk with your therapist. A therapist well-trained in working with betrayal trauma can introduce tools and interventions to help you slowly and gently build your internal capacity for handling your new reality. In time, you will emerge from your numbed state of shock and feel more present and connected.

∼

FOR YOUR CONSIDERATION

Journal Prompt

Shock is the brain's effort to protect you from information and events too overwhelming to deal with in the moment. In what ways have you experienced shock? Do you feel like you are in shock, have come out of shock, or are moving in and out of shock?

3

CIRCUIT OVERLOAD

*I*n addition to shock, you may experience significant changes in your daily functioning. When you are trying to absorb overwhelming, life-changing information that has plunged you into pain, grief, and confusion, your "circuits" get overloaded, and sometimes they will temporarily short out.

According to a study of partners of sex addicts conducted by Barbara Steffens in 2006, 71% of betrayed partners demonstrate a severe level of functional impairment in major areas of life after the discovery of infidelity.

I went through my own story of betrayal trauma many years ago. When I was in the initial crisis after discovery, life felt surreal and I did odd, silly, and downright dangerous things. I accidentally sprayed my hair with hairspray instead of mousse and dried it upside down into a strange and shocking Mohawk. I ran out of gas on the side of the road and had to be rescued by a friend because I couldn't figure out what to do next. I couldn't decide what to name my new kittens so I named them Black Cat and Grey Cat. I had too many "almost" car accidents to count. I lay awake until 7 a.m. having panic attacks. I shaved just one leg (many times). I rode my bike into oncoming traffic. I went through multiple cell phones (dropped in glasses of soda, puddles, orange juice). I lost my two indoor cats outdoors (I eventually found them). In general, I was short-tempered, tired, teary, and couldn't concentrate.

Here are some things betrayed partners frequently experience during the first few months after discovery:

- Forgetting things
- Clumsiness, accidents
- Sleeplessness or a desire to sleep all the time
- Difficulty concentrating
- Mixing up words when talking
- Inability to complete small tasks
- Wanting to isolate
- Anxiety, panic attacks, overwhelming fear
- Unstoppable crying or the inability to cry
- Anger, rage, or frustration
- Depression
- Racing thoughts or an inability to "turn your mind off"
- Intrusive thoughts of real or imagined scenes of our partner's sexual behavior
- Twitching eyes, legs, arms
- Loss of appetite or increase in appetite
- Headaches/migraines
- Body aches
- Feeling numb, robotic, or disconnected
- Sour or churning stomach
- Guilt or shame
- Thoughts of suicide or self-harm
- Frequent illness

During this initial stage, *whatever* you are feeling and experiencing, you are normal and others have experienced the same. You are on a wild emotional ride and betrayed partners have reported an incredible variety of feelings and experiences during this time. Be patient and gentle with yourself and do not expect more from yourself than is possible during this early period. Your body is handling more than normal and is overwhelmed. You may be searching for the right thing to do or an action to take, but what you really need is kindness, patience, realistic expectations, and lots of self-compassion.

FOR YOUR CONSIDERATION

Adjusting Expectations Exercise

1. Go back to the list of symptoms above. Put a check next to each one that applies to you. Write in any other symptoms you are experiencing that are not on the list.

2. Now take a few minutes to consider that for a while your ability to do what you normally would is going to be limited. Are you still expecting the same things from yourself? Are you putting pressure on yourself, or using your inner voice to criticize and scold yourself for not being able to "do life" the way you did before the betrayal?

3. Write a short letter to yourself about the expectations you have for yourself right now. How will you be more patient and kind to yourself? What will it mean to have expectations that are realistic and compassionate during this time? Where do you need to say no to others to take care of yourself?

4

EMOTIONAL ROLLERCOASTER

*A*fter discovery, you will find yourself suddenly riding an emotional rollercoaster of extreme and rapidly changing thoughts and feelings. One minute you'll feel hopeful and think you are doing well. The next minute you'll feel that your world is ending and you are falling apart. You may hate your partner one moment, and the next moment feel that you love him or her deeply. You may go to bed feeling like you want to stay in the relationship and to work things through, but wake up looking for the quickest route out the door. These rapid shifts from hope to despair, calm to rage, certainty to confusion, and fear to stability can make you feel like you are losing your sanity. On top of this, each strong emotion and reaction feels incredibly real and true while it is moving through you.

This is all normal. Betrayed partners have lots of big feelings about the betrayal, lots of confusion about the way forward. The human brain can only process one emotion at a time. That is why it can seem like your feelings change in a split second. This is your brain processing emotions in turn so that each one can be felt and moved through your body.

Hold Your Feelings Loosely

During this phase, one of the things that my clients and I talk about is how to hold their feelings loosely. This means allowing yourself to feel the feeling, noticing it, naming it, and allowing it to move through you without attaching to it. You may find yourself thinking, *You know, I was feeling calm, but then I thought about when I found those hotel receipts in my husband's wallet and now I am really angry.* This thought process may sound too simple, but it works, because, by noticing and naming what is happening, you give yourself permission to feel your feelings and you validate your reality.

Conversely, holding tightly to your feelings means attaching to and acting on a feeling before you have waited to see if that feeling is true and lasting or something that is just passing through. When you hold too tightly, you are likely to act on the feeling rather than thinking through what is best for you and your family.

I was talking with one of my clients about how to hold her feelings more loosely and she said something incredibly honest and enlightening: "It feels powerful to make a decision. Any decision. I don't even care what it is. It gets me out of feeling helpless. I want to *do something* even if it is the wrong thing or something I'll regret later."

This urge to act is strong for betrayed partners because they want to escape the pain and uncertainty as fast as possible. They are looking for ways to relieve their discomfort. Unfortunately, betrayed partners coping with the aftermath of betrayal can make poor decisions that do more harm than good to themselves and their families. The simple reality is that during this beginning stage of healing, most betrayed partners don't know where they will land emotionally after gathering information and processing what has happened.

Avoiding Needless Chaos

The more tightly you hold on to your feelings during this stage, the bigger and wilder the emotional rollercoaster ride will be, and the more chaos you will invite into your life. For example, if you wake up one morning feeling hopeless and wanting out of your relationship, holding tightly to your feelings may involve telling your spouse you are done, calling the divorce lawyer, and cancelling your couple's therapy session. However, that afternoon you may notice that you no longer feel so desperate to leave the relationship. Instead, you may feel some hope that perhaps you and your spouse can work it out. At that point, you will regret the steps you took in the morning and wish that you hadn't rushed into action.

Holding tightly to your feelings invites chaos into your life and causes you to expend a lot of emotional, physical, and mental energy on thoughts and feelings that are rapidly changing. These thoughts and feelings, while big and strong, are often temporary. They will shift and change over time.

The many feelings moving through your body are your brain's way of trying to process what has happened and sort through it to determine the way forward. Instead of grabbing a particular feeling and going with it, try telling yourself, "Right now I feel like I want out of the relationship, but I don't know if this is the decision that is best for me. So, for now I'm going to notice how I feel and I'm going to wait and see what happens with that. It's OK for me to not know what decision to make today."

～

FOR YOUR CONSIDERATION

Journal Prompt

Riding the emotional rollercoaster of sexual betrayal can be confusing and chaotic because your feelings change so rapidly. Think of a time when you attached to your emotions as they were happening and made decisions or took action based on that.

- What were you feeling?
- What behaviors did you engage in based on those feelings?
- What were the results?

- Were there negative consequences such as increased chaos, increased conflict, or increased pain?

Now think of a time when you were able to hold your feelings loosely, a time when you knew you were having a strong response to something but also knew that it was temporary and your feelings about it might change.

- Were you able to feel your feelings but not act on them in an impulsive way?
- What were you feeling?
- What happened?
- Were there positive consequences of being aware of your feelings but standing outside of them and waiting for them to pass or change?

5

CONNECTING THE DOTS

*A*fter discovering betrayal, you are likely to experience a period when you are flooded with memories and emotions as you begin to connect the dots about lies and secrets in your relationship. Past niggling feelings that something was wrong will unexpectedly resurface as you fill in the missing pieces.

That anniversary trip to Hawaii when he disappeared for an afternoon with no good explanation... Was he with a prostitute? The lack of sexual interest on her part... Is that because she'd been with him? The many times he told you he had to go downstairs and do work on the computer... Was he looking at porn and masturbating? The times you received extravagant gifts for no good reason... Was this because your partner felt guilty?

Consider Elaine, who recently found out about her husband's history of affairs. "I just figured out the other day that when I was in the hospital having surgery, my husband left the hospital and went to be with his mistress. I wondered at the time why he wasn't staying with me. I begged him to stay because I was in so much pain and needed him, but he said he couldn't and left. He went to be with her."

As the memories flood in, lines connect one dot to another. Signs and indications that weren't clear before now seem glaringly obvious. Shock, grief, and rage roll in like waves during this phase because each memory or realization feels like another brand new betrayal.

These realizations and connections often come at random times. You can be standing on line at the grocery store and suddenly two plus two becomes four. You can overhear a snippet of conversation and suddenly a piece of information will slide into place and reveal that *this* must mean *that.*

During this period, it is important to stick with the facts of what you know. Because your fear is running high and your body is in a state of hyper-vigilance, it is easy to create dots that don't exist or to connect dots that don't belong together. One way to help yourself with this is to stay focused on processing what you *do know* rather than what you might not know. Sometimes the search for more information is simply a way of distracting ourselves from facing the pain of what we already know.

This phase of connecting the dots can feel unending, as though the revelations will never stop coming, but there is an end to it. As you go through this stage, remember to use your tools of talking with supportive others, working with your therapist, journaling, crying, breathing, and being gentle and kind with yourself. This phase of recovery is a finite phenomenon, and eventually these new stabs of betrayal will stop. When they do, you will begin to truly heal.

FOR YOUR CONSIDERATION

Journal Prompt
What dots have you connected since the discovery of betrayal in your relationship? What has suddenly made sense to you that was unclear before?

Can you tell the difference between pieces of factual information that are connecting and creating new understanding versus times when your fear escalates and creates imagined connections that are not real? How are these two experiences different?

6

MY WHOLE RELATIONSHIP IS A LIE

*A*long with memories flooding in and connecting dot to dot you may feel as if nothing about your relationship can be trusted. As the scope and depth of the lying becomes clear, the betrayal deepens. The hurt about the lying and the secrets often feels more profound than the hurt from the sexual behaviors. I often picture the sexual behaviors as a tree and the lies and secrets as a complex root system winding its way deep into the soil of the relationship. As a result, it can feel as though the foundation of your entire relationship is permeated with lies and betrayal.

One of my clients said to me, "When I found out about my husband's behavior, he became creepy to me." She explained that she didn't know who he was, didn't understand how he could do what he had done. She thought she knew him and found that she really didn't, and that felt creepy to her. She had built a life with someone she thought she knew, but didn't, because he had a hidden second life. This realization makes it hard to separate the good from the bad in the relationship, and furthers the feeling that everything is now tainted by untruths and secrets.

When 'All Bad' Feels Safer

It is tempting to mentally and emotionally throw the relational baby out with the bathwater. It seems safer to decide that your partner is a bad person than to try to come to grips with your partner being a good person who has done bad things. If he or she is all bad, you can protect yourself by pulling away and walling off. If he or she is all bad, things are more predictable. You can expect disappointment, and by expecting it, you aren't hurt so deeply when it comes.

The same is true with your relationship. If you decide that the entire relationship was a lie, it seems safer to simply abandon it. It is far more painful and confusing to acknowledge that your spouse really does love you, that you have positive and wonderful memories together, and that he or she has come through for you in significant ways in the past, than it is to walk away. If these positive things are true, it makes the betrayal hurt even more. So, it is tempting to decide that the whole relationship was a lie, and to discard the loving and positive parts of it.

The downside to painting with the "all bad" brush, is that you lose more than if you do the hard work of sorting through what has happened. You temporarily stay safer emotionally and you have less risk of more pain, but there is a tradeoff. You lose the truth of your relationship, and you lose the good of your relationship. Most relationships, no matter how fraught, have positive aspects to them. So, if you decide the whole relationship is one big lie, you end up trading one form of dishonesty for another.

Sorting the Relationship

Here is what I tell my clients when they get to this point: Think of your relationship as a giant junk heap. It is piled high and God only knows what the heck is buried in there. Over the coming weeks, you and your partner are going to sort through the pile. In it you may find some things that are nasty, shocking, and probably heartbreaking. You will have to separate those out from the rest and determine what they mean for you. You will also find some treasures, things that are precious to you, surprises that remind you of why you love this person. There will be sudden bursts of nostalgia, and maybe joy. Again, you will need separate these out to determine what meaning they hold for you.

As you sort through the pile you will eventually gain clarity and understanding about what has happened, what it means for you, and what the way forward looks like. You will see good parts of the relationship that you want to hold on to, and dysfunctional parts that you want to change. You might decide to stay in the relationship for now to see what recovery has to offer. You might find that you need to leave the relationship. Whatever path you choose, if you can wait until you've sorted the pile, you will gain more clarity and make better decisions for yourself.

∾

FOR YOUR CONSIDERATION

Journal Prompt

Have you found yourself unconsciously deciding that your spouse is "all bad" and the relationship is "all lies"? If so, what do you *gain* by doing this? For example, does it make you feel safer? Do things feel more predictable?

What do you *lose* by deciding your spouse and relationship are "all bad" or "all lies"? What good traits of your spouse or good aspects of your relationship get lost or ignored? When you lose these positive traits how does it impact you? How do you feel about yourself, your spouse and your relationship as a result?

7

SHAME ON WHO?

*W*hen you discover betrayal in your relationship, you may feel overwhelmed by shame. Usually, this shame is rooted in a secret fear that some lack in you has caused your spouse to go outside the relationship sexually. You might fear that if others find out about the cheating, you will be judged as an inadequate spouse or partner. You might fear that your relationships with family and close friends will suffer. You might also worry that if your spouse is diagnosed as a sex addict, he or she will be labeled a pervert.

Most betrayed partners feel terribly isolated with their shame, as though they have a secret they can't share. One of my clients put it this way: "You aren't connecting with people anymore because you are no longer like them. You have huge issues with isolation, confusion, and rage."

Shame motivates many betrayed partners to keep the infidelity, the sexual addiction, and accompanying behaviors secret. They don't feel they can tell those around them about what has been discovered and what they are going through. As a result, they inadvertently participate in keeping secrets. Recognizing this, early recovery emphasizes the need to reach out to supportive others. If a betrayed partner feels that she or he cannot tell anyone and instead suffers in

29

silence, this perpetuates the unfaithful partner's veil of lies and secrecy, and continues the pain of betrayal.

At the other extreme, some betrayed partners essentially grab a bullhorn and broadcast their dirty laundry to as many people as possible. Often, this public shaming is a subtle (or not so subtle) form of revenge, driven by the anger they feel about being betrayed. It is also often an unconscious effort to repudiate the shame they feel. It is a very human response to manage feelings of shame by shaming others.

Unfortunately, this behavior does not alleviate shame. Even worse, it can create relational damage that may take years to fix. For example, one of my clients told her family about her spouse's behavior before stopping to consider how her family would respond. Five years into a solid recovery, her family still wants nothing to do with her spouse. This puts an incredible strain on her as she balances her relationship with her spouse and her relationship with her family.

The need to overcome shame and isolation in a healthy and productive way is why it is so important for you to seek outside help and get plugged into a community of support. You need people who understand the betrayal trauma you have experienced, and can guide you into a process of dealing with and healing from what has happened. You need to sit in a room with other individuals who have experienced what you are experiencing, where you can tell the shameful secrets and find out that in telling them your shame begins to lift and dissipate.

FOR YOUR CONSIDERATION

Shame Picture Exercise
1. Draw a picture of the shame you feel about the betrayal. If your shame has a color, what color is it? If your shame has a shape, what shape is it? If your shame has a texture, what texture is it? Is it solid, liquid, gas, heavy, soft, prickly, etc.?

2. Now that you have a picture of your shame, sit back and consider it. Does this shame belong to you? Is it something you want to keep and carry, or would you like to release it?

3. Sometimes, keeping the shame can have secondary benefits that we are not consciously aware of, such as keeping us from taking risks with others. Are there any hidden benefits to carrying your shame? What would you gain from releasing the shame?

4. When you are ready, take the picture of shame that you drew and symbolically release it in some way. I have had clients burn the picture, send it off on a piece of bark in a stream, bury it, or tear it up and throw it away. Do whatever feels right for you.

8

STRANGER IN THE MIRROR

*W*hen I was in the initial shock of dealing with betrayal trauma, I barely recognized myself. The competent, funny, focused woman I knew was gone, and in her place was a shattered, anxious, broken stranger. This stranger cried all the time, raged like a maniac, was exhausted and depressed, couldn't concentrate, and felt desperate. I looked in the mirror and thought: *What is happening to me? How did I become this person?*

In the aftermath of betrayal, it can feel as though someone else has taken over your emotional and physical body. Suddenly you don't recognize yourself. You've never had panic attacks before and now you have them daily. You've never screamed at your spouse the way you screamed at him or her this morning, or felt the kind of rage and hatred you've felt since finding out. You've never retreated from life before, but now you are unable to face your day.

This abrupt change in who we know ourselves to be creates a double whammy of loss. Not only are we grieving the loss of who we thought our partner was, we are grieving the loss of ourselves. Unfortunately, it is often the best parts of ourselves that we have lost—the funny, playful, relaxed, open, generous parts. And what seems to be surfacing is a dark, anxious side we may not have known about. This can be very disorienting, as we no longer feel like we can count on ourselves. Our normal responses have gone missing and we are left with unpredictable and unfamiliar reactions.

A Hidden Gift

While this disorientation of the self is challenging and frightening, there is also, unbelievably, a hidden gift. The hidden gift is that we get to know ourselves much better. We become more aware of what we are capable of in both good ways and bad.

I learned that I can cope with more than I ever imagined, that I have reservoirs of strength and resilience that are there for me when I need them, that I make great decisions under fire, that I am able to walk through extremely painful situations with grace and dignity, that I am stubbornly persistent. I also learned I have deep wells of anger that I didn't know about before the betrayal. I can be mean, spiteful, and fight like an emotional street brawler. Worst of all, I can be wounded in ways that take a long time to heal.

We are all capable of glorious bravery and hideous damage. Part of being a mature adult is to be aware of both the dignity and depravity that reside within us. As a betrayed partner, you are in the middle of adversity right now. This means that you are automatically on a journey of imposed self-discovery. You may feel that you have lost your true self and don't know who you are anymore. The good news is that as you heal, you are going to discover new parts of yourself that you will treasure for the rest of your life.

FOR YOUR CONSIDERATION

Journal Prompt

In the aftermath of betrayal, it can feel as though someone has taken over your emotional and physical body. What parts of yourself do you feel you have lost touch with as a result of betrayal trauma? What parts of yourself are you discovering as a result of betrayal trauma?

.

9

BLOCKING IT OUT

*I*n the aftermath of learning about infidelity, one coping behavior that many betrayed partners employ is to block out what they have learned, sweeping it under the proverbial rug. This is different from putting aside your thoughts and feelings about what happened to pick the kids up from school, grocery shop, or meet a project deadline at work. That is a necessary, good, and helpful skill that enables you to continue to function.

What I'm talking about here is forgetting that your partner cheated or that your partner is a sex addict—forgetting the betrayals that were disclosed because it feels too daunting to live in that reality. As an example, my client Kim came in for her appointment and began to talk about how she used to feel when her spouse was acting out. She was talking about it as though it were long in the past, but her spouse had been sober for only two weeks. Another client, Mary, came in and reported that she and her spouse had unprotected sex the day before. When I reminded her that she was waiting for him to be tested for HIV and other STDs because he'd had unprotected sex with prostitutes, she looked at me in shock. She had forgotten all about that.

Tucking away such difficult, painful information is easy to do, and the temptation is oh so understandable. If you can be aware of the tendency to do this and work to stay grounded in reality, you will be better able to take care of and protect yourself.

When you block out information, you no longer know what you need, what boundaries are appropriate, how to protect yourself, or what the best course of action is, because you are operating without the full facts. It's like having one of your senses go missing. You can hear but not see, see but not smell, etc. It limits you.

To help yourself stay aware of what you know, I suggest using your journal to write things down, asking supportive friends to remind you if they see you forgetting things, and talking about what you have found out to help process and digest it. These and similar tools can help you stay grounded in your reality.

∾

FOR YOUR CONSIDERATION

Journal Prompt
What have you blocked out because it feels too overwhelming to face?

What is it like to bring this information into your awareness? What feelings come up?

Usually we block things out because they are troubling to us and feel like they are beyond our coping capacities. What support might you need to help you deal with and process the things that you have been blocking out?

10

I FEEL LIKE SUCH A FOOL

One of my clients brought in a collage she created representing her experience of betrayal trauma. In the center of her collage, in big block letters, she had pasted the words I'M A STUPID GIRL. When I asked her about this, she talked about feeling foolish for believing the lies her husband had told her.

She is not alone with this feeling. Every betrayed partner I have ever worked with has talked about feeling like a fool when they found out about their significant other's sexual behavior. Betrayed partners feel their trust in their spouse has been taken advantage of and used to hurt them. They feel shame for trusting someone untrustworthy. They are angry with themselves for giving the benefit of the doubt to someone who did not deserve it. They feel they should have known about the behaviors. They are unable to trust their partner and, even worse, they are unable to trust themselves.

What happens here is that rather than holding your significant other responsible for the lies and deceit in your relationship, you blame yourself for trusting him or her. When you do this, you are taking the blame of the betrayal and turning it against yourself. You are blaming yourself for what is actually your partner's responsibility. You are carrying your partner's shame and guilt.

Here is another option: Hold your unfaithful partner responsible.

Instead of turning on yourself with your pain and meanly calling yourself a fool, you can hold your spouse accountable. You can place responsibility for the secrets and lies on the person who perpetuated them. When you do this, you recognize that your trust in your partner and your hope for the relationship came from a good part of you. It does not mean you were foolish to hope for the best and to give your partner the benefit of the doubt. In fact, this kind of goodwill is what makes relationships work.

Instead of calling yourself a fool, you may need to recognize that you feel sad, hurt, betrayed, and disappointed. Sometimes it is easier to get angry with yourself than to face other, even more painful feelings. However, holding your partner accountable rather than blaming yourself is a much kinder way to deal with your feelings. Plus, it places responsibility for the betrayal in the correct place.

～

FOR YOUR CONSIDERATION

You Are Not a Fool Exercise
Write a short note to the part of you that feels like a fool. Write this note from the part of you that is able to show up as a nurturing parent to yourself. What do you want to say to the part that feels like a fool? What does that part of you need to hear? How can you affirm your ability to trust and see the positive in your partner as it existed before you learned about the betrayal?

IS IT MY FAULT

*I*t. Is. Not. Your. Fault. You did not cause your partner's infidelity.

Most betrayed partners carry the burden of the same secret fear —*that some lack in them caused their significant other to seek sexual experiences outside of the relationship.* The fear sounds something like this:

- If I were thinner, had bigger breasts, was taller, had tighter thighs, were younger, had a prettier face, etc., then he would not be looking at pornography on the Internet.
- If I were a better husband, paid more attention, earned more money, was a better leader, etc., then she would not be involved with these other men.
- If I had sex more often, had been willing to be more experimental, had said yes to that threesome, had participated in using pornography, etc., then he would not be having sex with random strangers.

Sound familiar? Sexual betrayal triggers pre-existing doubts and insecurities. We immediately wonder if it is our fault that our partner went outside the boundaries of our relationship. This fear gnaws at us, and, though we desperately want it not to be true, deep inside we think that maybe it is.

Our surrounding culture does not help us with this issue, especially if we are female. Television, the Internet, movies, and songs all tout the age-old theme that it is the woman's fault if her man strays. I cannot count the number of clients (especially the women) who have told me that when they finally had the courage to tell someone—a friend, a pastor, a family member—the first question they were asked was how much sex they were providing. This culture of blame increases the shame for betrayed partners and the feeling that they are in some way responsible for their significant other's behavior.

Knowing in Your Heart

Getting grounded in the reality that we are not responsible for our partner's behavior takes some time. We are usually able to grasp this principle intellectually, but it takes a while for it to travel to our hearts and to *feel* true. The good news is that the thoughts we choose to tell ourselves determine how we feel, not the other way around. Twelve-step fellowships use the slogans "act as if" and "fake it till you make it" to put this principle into action. The idea is that when you change your thinking and behavior, eventually your feelings follow.

This means you can make a conscious choice to believe that you are not responsible for your partner's behavior, and to live that truth. If you instead choose to live the lie—that you caused the betrayal—that lie will feed your insecurity and drive you to behaviors that are not helpful. If you live the truth that you are a delightful, lovable, valuable individual and you did not cause the betrayal, you will be better able to choose your *response* to things rather than simply *reacting*. Soon, you will *feel* the stability and freedom of knowing that your partner's cheating behaviors are separate from you.

One of the things that helps betrayed partners understand they are not responsible for their partner's behavior is sitting in group therapy or 12-step meetings with other betrayed partners. When they hear others' stories, they are able to see clearly who is and who is not responsible for the cheating. Seeing this in others helps them see their own situation more clearly.

Another element that may help you see beyond yourself as the cause of your partner's cheating is learning about your partner's history. Often, your partner's sexual behaviors were present in previous relationships. If he or she is sexually addicted, the behaviors may have begun all the way back in childhood or early adolescence, long before the two of you even met.

As the betrayed partner, you have responsibility for your part of the relational dynamic that exists between you and your significant other. And you have responsibility for what happens in the relationship today and how the two of you go forward. However, you are not responsible for your partner choosing to betray you.

The Unconscious Tradeoff

Let's talk about what you might gain by blaming yourself for your partner's behavior. And yes, I know that may sound strange. You may think, *what benefit could I possibly be getting from this?* Well, in my personal and clinical experience there is a payoff to be gained from this belief.

Here it is. Here's what you get from blaming yourself: You get to keep the dearly held hope that you can somehow control your partner's behavior. Let me say it again: The deep fear that you have caused the betrayal is tied very closely to your hope that you can control the betrayal. If some lack or deficiency in you is causing your partner to stray, then you can fix that; you can do something about that. But if your partner's behavior does not have anything to do with you, you are confronted with your powerlessness over his or her actions. And it is very hard to admit that you are powerless in the face of something that is causing you so much pain.

The desire to find a way to try to control and prevent further betrayal is a very human one. Believing you have caused the betrayal is a way to try to manage the pain and uncertainty it is bringing into your life. It is very hard to give up this belief because it means facing the fact that the person solely responsible for the sexual behavior is your significant other. He or she is the only one who can do the work necessary to ensure that the betrayal stops and the damage to your relationship is meaningfully and fully repaired.

When you let go of the fear-based belief that you have caused the betrayal, you also surrender your belief that you can fix or control it. This frees you from the false hope offered by control, and opens you to the true hope that comes from letting go.

There is freedom in recognizing that you cannot control your spouse. You are free to release him or her and to focus on living your own life in the best way possible. You get to reclaim your power and use your energy to help yourself. You no longer believe that your partner's behaviors are in any way a referendum on your lovability or worthiness. You can stay connected to your own inherent worth and to live out of that lushly green place inside of yourself, rather than wandering through the desert of personal despair and self-blame.

FOR YOUR CONSIDERATION

Journal Prompt
Take a few minutes to list the reasons why you may think your partner's betrayal is your fault.

Now sit back and consider your list. Is there anything on that list that has contributed to challenges in your relationship? Are there things on the list that you cognitively know are not true but emotionally you struggle with?

What is it like to acknowledge that although you may have contributed to challenges in the relationship, you are not responsible for your partner's betraying behavior?

Fear and Freedom Exercise

Review the following sentence:
The deep fear that you have caused the betrayal is tied very closely to the hope that you can control the betrayal.

Is there a part of you that holds on to blaming yourself in order to not feel powerless or helpless about your pain? What feelings arise when you confront the reality that you do not have the power to keep your partner from betraying you?

Allow yourself to fully face and articulate the fears you have. These fears are a normal part of dealing with betrayal trauma.

Review the following sentence:
There is freedom in recognizing that you do not have power over your partner. You are free to release him or her and to focus on living your own life in the best way possible. When you do this, you are set free to use your energy to help yourself.

What is your reaction to this? In what ways does letting go of blaming yourself set you free to focus on your own healing and growth? What emotional space does it open up in your life? Draw a picture of what this freedom feels like.

LOSS AND GRIEF

*D*iscovering sexual betrayal plunges you into loss and grief. Suddenly you are faced with more losses than you can count. Loss of trust in your partner, loss of trust in yourself, loss of the relationship you thought you had, and loss of your dreams for the future.

Elisabeth Kübler-Ross, a pioneer in the study of grief and loss associated with death and dying, identified five stages of grief. Over time, these five stages have become recognized as the stages that people dealing with all types of trauma, including the trauma of sexual betrayal, go through. The stages are: denial, anger, bargaining, depression, and acceptance. These stages are not linear.

For example, you may begin your day telling yourself that at least your partner didn't have sex with a live person (bargaining and denial stages). A little later you might remember walking in on your partner looking at Internet pornography and you might feel tremendous rage, disgust, and shame (anger stage). That afternoon you might feel lifeless, unmotivated, and exhausted (depression stage), while also feeling like you are beginning to understand more about sex addiction and why your partner has done the things that he or she has done (acceptance stage).

The stages of grief are a winding journey, skipping around in no particular order, doubling back on themselves and sometimes washing over you all at once. Grief is on its own schedule, rising inside of you at the most inconvenient times and places. If you can honor grief when it shows up and allow yourself to feel it despite how inconvenient and exhausting it can be, this will allow your emotions to be processed, helping you move through your grief and loss more quickly.

Understanding Acceptance

Let me clarify a bit about the stage of acceptance, as that word can feel triggering for some betrayed partners. Acceptance does not mean being OK with or excusing your partner's behavior. Instead, acceptance is about beginning to understand how your reality has shifted, and coming to grips with how to live well in your new reality.

After my divorce, I remember asking myself, "How do I build a life that I don't want?" I didn't want to be single again, bearing the wounds and scars of a traumatic marriage and divorce. That is not the reality I wanted, and for a long time I couldn't figure out how to build a life for myself based on a reality I didn't want. Over time, however, I put bits and pieces of a new life into place—a career I love and thrive in, a lovely home that is a place of rest and play, friends and family that nurture, support, and love me. This is what acceptance looks like. It comes bit by bit, and we move in and out of it as we discover what it means to have a full and generous life in the midst of new and often challenging circumstances.

Over the coming weeks, you are going to grieve the many losses resulting from your partner's betrayal. It is possible that the biggest losses will center around losing your sense of self, and losing the partner and relationship you thought you had.

Be gentle with yourself. Give yourself plenty of space to feel sad, to cry buckets of tears, and to talk with safe friends about what you have lost. Grief is an exhausting emotion, so you are going to be tired. Very tired. Patience with yourself and realistic expectations about what you can manage are needed. And because I don't think betrayed partners can hear this enough, I will say it here: This will not last forever. You are going to experience joy again. You are going to come out of this and you will once again feel happiness, contentment, gratitude, and openness. This is a dark tunnel you are passing through, but there is daylight at the end of it.

∽

FOR YOUR CONSIDERATION

Journal Prompt
Make a list of the things you have lost as a result of your partner's betrayal. Many of these losses may be temporary, but if you are experiencing them right now, put them on the list. These losses can be physical things (loss of money, loss of a much-anticipated trip, loss of a friend, loss of the sexual relationship) or emotional things (loss of safety, loss of joy, loss of trust).

Allow yourself the space to feel sadness and grief around these losses. Give yourself permission to cry, to call a friend, to request comfort from those close to you. In the same way someone needs support after the death of a loved one, you need support. You have experienced the death of the relationship you thought you had, and you are grieving in the same way as a person whose loved one died.

Grief Kit Exercise
One of the most important things you need while grieving is comfort. Make a list of items or actions that help you to feel comfort when you are sad and grief stricken. Some items might include: A hug from your best friend, your favorite sweatshirt and yoga pants, a warm bath, a long talk with your sister, petting your dog/cat, snuggling up under your favorite throw, being held, etc. There are no right or wrong

answers here. Each person is different, and what brings you comfort will be unique to you. Let yourself explore and name what you need to help you through this stage.

13

SUMMING UP

*A*s we come to the end of this book, I hope that you now have a better understanding of what is happening to you because of experiencing betrayal. I hope you have words and language to help you articulate to yourself and others the wild, chaotic, scary, and painful process you are in. I hope you feel validated. You are not crazy; nothing is wrong with you.

You are in the middle of an incredibly challenging circumstance and you are reacting in normal ways to the abnormal stressor of betrayal. Most of all, I hope you know that you are not alone. Many others have experienced betrayal trauma, and there is support, care, guidance, and wisdom available to help you navigate your way.

ACKNOWLEDGMENTS

∽

You would be amazed at what it takes to put a book like this out into the world. I certainly did not do this alone, and I am filled with gratitude for all the help and support I've had along the way. Here are some of the folks for whom I am particularly thankful.

Steve, my dear friend and writing group buddy who at this point probably has this book memorized and now knows far more about betrayal trauma than he ever wished to. Thank You.

Beth, Brooke, Julie, Cyndi, Andrea, Denise, Lynda, Kari, Laurie, and Heather (in memoriam), my gaggle of girlfriends who have traveled the bumpy road with me, laughed and cried with me, and *always* seen me. Thank You.

Mary, Bruce, Cheryl, Nan, Nichole and Kacey, the amazing team at the Center for Relational Recovery, who have taken over the care of our clients with excellence, wisdom, and commitment so I could step back and write. Thank You.

The women of the PartnerHope Focus Group who read the draft, gave insightful feedback, encouraged me, and generously spoke from their own experiences in the hope that others will greatly benefit. Thank You.

Scott Brassart, copyeditor extraordinaire, and book designers Joel Markquart and Polly Yakovich this book sings because of your help.

ABOUT THE AUTHOR

∾

Michelle D. Mays LPC, CSAT-S is the founder of PartnerHope, a comprehensive resource and online community offering authentic hope and practical help to those recovering from betrayal trauma.

She is also the founder and Clinical Director of the Center for Relational Recovery, serving individuals and couples struggling with sexual addiction, betrayal trauma, childhood trauma, and relationship issues. Michelle is in the process of writing a full-length book for partners of sex addicts due out soon.

Michelle is a Certified Sex Addiction Therapist and Supervisor trained under Dr. Patrick Carnes. She is also trained in Post Induction Therapy (for the treatment of relational trauma) by Pia Mellody. She is currently completing her certification in Emotionally Focused Therapy for couples. She is a Registered Supervisor with the state of Virginia and is licensed as a Professional Counselor in both Virginia and Washington DC.

On a personal note, here are a few things to know about Michelle. Snow makes her happy. Reading is her favorite. She hates asparagus. The beach is the happiest place on earth. Her siblings and sibling-in-laws make her laugh out loud. She regularly refers to her dog as "her lab-ness." She would rather not be bored. Ever. A night out with friends can't be beat. Music makes life worth living. Interior design is her secret fixation and she wants to come back as Joanna Gaines in her next life. A morning spent writing on her sun porch is the best morning ever. A tent and a campfire almost always end in tears (usually from laughter but sometimes not). And she *really* wishes she could teleport.

MORE HOPE AND HELP

~

For more hope and help in recovering from betrayal trauma visit PartnerHope.com. There you can sign up to receive a weekly blog post from Michelle, and to be part of the "testing hope" membership group when the resource site goes live in 2018.

71502050R00038

Made in the USA
Middletown, DE
25 April 2018